I Just Want to Be Healed

"You already are" — *Jesus*

By Dan Bean

Beloved International
3936 Fox Ridge Blvd
Wesley Chapel, FL 33543
(813) 779-8777
www.BelovedInternational.US
Beloved@BelovedInternational.US

Published in the United States of America

Thank you to Veronica, my amazing wife and ministry partner, who provided
tremendous assistance. Thanks, also, to Lisa McCarthy and Max Carroll for
your amazing help editing the text.

Paperback: ISBN 979-898988340-0
Electronic: ISBN 979-898988341-7

I Just Want to Be Healed

Contents

Preface 1

I Just Want to Be Healed 3

1. The Source of Life 5

2. Obstacles to Receiving Healing 9

3. Hindrance # 1 11

4. Hindrance # 2 15

5. Hindrance # 3 17

6. Hindrance # 4 21

7. Hindrance # 5 25

8. Hindrance # 6 29

9. Hindrance # 7 33

10. Hindrance # 8 37

11. Hindrance # 9 41

12. Revelation is the Key 45

13. Faith Doesn't Look at the Natural 47

14. Look to Jesus 49

15. How do I Receive Healing? 51

16. You Already are Healed 55

17. You Can Receive Healing Today 57

18. Act on God's Word to You 59

19. Have a Listening Heart 61

20. Deal With the Root Cause 65

21. Ways to Receive Healing 69

22. Jesus Gave us Authority 75

23. Staying Healed 79

Here's How to Pray 81

About the Author 83

Preface

The last time I went to the doctor was in August of 1997. At the time of this writing, that was over twenty-six years ago. No, I don't have super human genes or keep a strict diet; I just have a revelation of God's love. Jesus healed me 2,000 years ago and I have learned how to enjoy the gift He has given me.

There have been many times that I have felt in my body the symptoms of pain and sickness, but by God's grace I have resisted all of them. I believe God loves it when we enjoy health. He died so that we can live as one of His children and have abundant life, and I want you to enjoy God's quality of life, also.

The principles in this book have given me the freedom to have and enjoy health, and I want you to have the same. I pray that you receive a revelation of divine healing from the Holy Spirit as you apply what you are about to read.

I Just Want to Be Healed

I spent twenty-five years building and remodeling houses. While on the job one day, I felt very sick to my stomach. I was weak and couldn't stay focused. I sat down on my lunch cooler and hung my head toward the ground. With my eyes closed, wondering if I would make it through the rest of the day, a scene played through my thoughts.

I saw myself sitting on the edge of a cobbled street in ancient Jerusalem with a parade of people flowing down the dusty pathway. Jesus came to the side of the road where I sat and asked me what I wanted. I lifted my head and told Him, "I just want to be healed." He reached out His hand to me and said, "You already are." My stomach felt much better after that experience, and I finished out the day.

That was just one of the many experiences I have had regarding healing. I know that Jesus has already provided healing for every one of us. Not only did He take our place on the cross for all our sins, He was also beaten for all our sickness and disease. Every illness and pain already has a cure—it's Jesus.

The goal of this book is to help you know how to finally receive healing. Whether you need healing or you want to help someone else receive healing, I hope this book helps you get there. Healing is not complicated or difficult. God wants you well. Healing is His idea. He sent Jesus to take your place so that you can be healthy. How do I know it's God's will for you to be healed? Because I know He loves you.

Many people underestimate or don't comprehend God's love. It is a driving force. Everything that God has done for us is from love. Love is more than a description of our relationship; His love is a constant flow of power toward us. Ephesians 1:19a says, "*And what is the exceeding greatness of His power toward us who believe.*" His love is a never-ending flow of power that is constantly seeking ways to prosper, protect, and provide for us. It is waiting for us to receive it.

The Father's love is like a power station. The power is produced and sent to the user before the need arises. All you have to do is plug into a receptacle to access the power available. Plugging in does not initiate the production of power. It is already there waiting for us to access it. God's love for us is far greater than any modern power plant. He is actively involved in all areas of our life. His foresight made power available before we knew that we even needed it. Christ provided healing many years ago. We are not waiting for it to be produced. God is waiting for us to tap into it. It was God's awesome love that saw our needs beforehand and made healing available for us to access now.

Chapter 1

The Source of Life

Love, which is God Himself, wanted to make sure that we could live long, healthy lives. Sickness originated from Satan and came to mankind when Adam and Eve sinned. Jesus came to destroy the works of the enemy and to give us His quality of life.

> *The thief does not come except to steal, and to kill, and to destroy. I have come that they may have life, and that they may have it more abundantly.*
>
> John 10:10

Jesus came to give us life! The Greek word for "life" is "*zoe.*" It is defined as, "God's quality and quantity of life". It means to live like God lives, with His abundance and exuberance. It is joy, health, and energy for every day of your life! According to Romans 8:11; this life is in you.

> *But if the Spirit of Him who raised Jesus from the dead dwells in you, He who raised Christ from the dead will also give life to your mortal bodies through His Spirit who dwells in you.*
>
> Romans 8:11

Every branch on a tree has life because it is connected to the source of life, the tree. We have life in us because we have the Holy Spirit in us. We don't have to search for life, we already have it. Because the Holy Spirit, who is life, dwells within us, we have His life working in us. His life causes our mortal bodies to have the same quality and quantity of life that He has. Yes, we can live free from sickness and disease because we have the source of life within us. Unfortunately, many of the branches that are connected to Christ are not receiving this life because they are blocked by all kinds of wrong thinking. Neither you nor the devil can stop God's love for you, but it can be hindered by lack of knowledge.

> *My people are destroyed for lack of knowledge...*
>
> Hosea 4:6

People aren't enjoying life because they don't know they can. Years of wrong teaching have kept them from receiving God's love. Religion often produces doubt in God's willingness and ability; then those doubts block the flow of God's power. In their own pride, they attempt to receive healing by their own means. Eventually, their efforts lead to unbelief and they say there never was any power flowing. Just because you may not have experienced God's healing power does not mean God doesn't want you healed.

You can tell exactly what God's will is by looking at what Jesus did throughout His ministry.

> *Then Jesus answered and said to them, "Most assuredly, I say to you, the Son can do nothing of Himself, but what He sees the Father do; for whatever He does, the Son also does in like manner."*
>
> John 5:19

Jesus is the perfect picture of God's will, especially in regards to healing. Everything He did demonstrates God's will for us. Jesus always did the will of the Father. He was never disobedient, presumptuous, or out of line. If He did it, then we know it is what the Father wanted done.

Throughout the Gospels, we see Jesus doing the will of the Father by healing the sick. Many heard about Jesus healing people and went to Him to be healed. Everyone that came was set free from sickness. Some refused to believe that Jesus was sent by God and called it a work of the devil. But the ones, who did believe were healed. Healing really is simple. If you believe Jesus can and will heal, you will receive.

I Just Want to Be Healed

Chapter 2

Obstacles to Receiving Healing

Religion has invented thousands of ways to doubt that God will heal you. Let me list a few:

1. God doesn't do that anymore.
2. It isn't God's will to heal you.
3. God must be teaching you something.
4. My suffering will bring God Glory.
5. You have a generational curse.
6. You have sin in your life.
7. It's your own fault.
8. You haven't done enough to be healed.
9. You just don't have enough faith.

All of these hinder people from receiving healing; however, faith is dependent on knowing that it is God's will to heal you. If you doubt God, then you disqualify yourself from His promises. You can't have faith to be healed when you doubt that He wants to heal you. This way of thinking takes your focus away from the finished work of Jesus and onto yourself. The devil wants to keep us from plugging into God's power and receiving what is already available. Instead of creating doubts, we need to remove all the hindrances and establish that it is God's desire for you to live in health. It has always been God's will for you to be healed. He has never changed and His power is always toward us.

So let's deal with some of the doubts that keep people from receiving.

Chapter 3

Hindrance # 1

Some say,
"God doesn't do that anymore."

What exactly are they talking about when they say this? Are they referring to miracles? Healings? Answered prayer? Do they think that God had one will for the Old Testament and another for the New Testament? Is God schizophrenic? Did He change along the way? No! God has never changed. If it was God's will to heal in the Old Testament, it is God's will to heal in the New Testament.

"For I am the LORD, I do not change; ..."
Malachi 3:6

Jesus Christ is the same yesterday, today, and forever.
Hebrews 13:8

God didn't use miracles to build the church and then stop using miracles once the church was established. He is still doing miracles, healing people, and answering prayer. The reason some believe it has stopped is because they aren't experiencing it. Religion caused them to stop focusing on their relationship with Jesus and put their attention on doctrine and methods. They lost their fellowship with God and began following man's traditions. These customs nullified the Word, and these people stopped seeing the miraculous.

He answered and said to them, "Well did Isaiah prophesy of you hypocrites, as it is written: 'This people honors Me with their lips, but their heart is far from Me and in vain they worship Me, teaching as doctrines the commandments of men.' For laying aside the commandment of God, you hold the tradition of men— the washing of pitchers and cups, and many other such things you do." He said to them," All too well you reject the commandment of God, that you may keep your tradition. . . . making the word of God of no effect through your tradition which you have handed down. And many such things you do."

Mark 7:6-9, 13

Jesus performed more miracles than could be recorded in books (John 21:25); but He isn't the only one that can perform miracles. He told His disciples that His work would continue, through them, after He was gone.

"Most assuredly, I say to you, he who believes in Me, the works that I do he will do also; and greater works than these he will do, because I go to My Father. And whatever you ask in My name, that I will do, that the Father may be glorified in the Son. If you ask anything in My name, I will do it."

John 14:12-14

He didn't change, man changed. God is still healing today through believers. If you will connect with God in your heart, He will reveal Himself to you and demonstrate how much He loves you. God is love. He has always been love. And His love has always been toward us.

Beloved, let us love one another, for love is of God; and everyone who loves is born of God and knows God. He who does not love does not know God, for God is love. In this the love of God was manifested toward us, that God has sent His only begotten Son into the world, that we might live through Him. In this is love, not that we loved God, but that He loved us and sent His Son to be the propitiation (The one who took our sin upon Himself, thus making us right before God.) *for our sins.*

1 John 4:7-10

Chapter 4

Hindrance # 2

Some say,
"It isn't God's will to heal you."

The best way to determine God's will is to look at Jesus. He said He only did the will of the Father.

> *For I have come down from heaven, not to do My own*
> *will, but the will of Him who sent Me.*
> > *John 6:38*

If you want to know the Father's will, look at what Jesus did. In Matthew chapter 8, Jesus cleansed the leper, healed the centurion's servant, rebuked the fever from Peter's mother-in-law, cast out many demons, and healed all who were sick. In verse 17 Matthew writes, He did all this *"that it might be fulfilled which was spoken by Isaiah the prophet, saying: 'He Himself took our infirmities and bore our sickness.' "*

Jesus healed all these people to prove that healing is God's will. John also wrote about Jesus doing the Father's will.

> *Then Jesus answered and said to them, "Most assuredly,*
> *I say to you, the Son can do nothing of Himself, but what*
> *He sees the Father do; for whatever He does, the Son*
> *also does in like manner.*
> > *John 5:19*

I can of Myself do nothing. As I hear, I judge; and My judgment is righteous, because I do not seek My own will but the will of the Father who sent Me.

John 5: 30

Everything Jesus did was the Father's desire. Everyone that He healed, God wanted them healed. Since Jesus healed everyone that came to Him, then we know that it is God's will to heal all. Jesus was only asked one time if it was His will to heal; He replied that He was willing and healed the man.

And behold, a leper came and worshiped Him, saying, "Lord, if You are willing, You can make me clean." Then Jesus put out His hand and touched him, saying, "I am willing; be cleansed." Immediately his leprosy was cleansed.

Matthew 8:2-3

Chapter 5

Hindrance # 3

Some say,
"God must be teaching you something."

The Holy Spirit is our teacher, not sickness.

> *But the Helper, the Holy Spirit, whom the Father will*
> *send in My name, He will teach you all things, and bring*
> *to your remembrance all things that I said to you.*
>
> John 14:26

Throughout life we will go through tests. They help us develop character and spiritual strength. Everyone thinks of Job when the subject of being tested comes up, he was not tested by God—he was tried by Satan. God never engages in evil to teach us.

> *Let no one say when he is tempted, "I am tempted by*
> *God"; for God cannot be tempted by evil, nor does He*
> *Himself tempt anyone.*
>
> James 1:13

Just because you are going through tough times doesn't mean it was ordained by God. The devil targets righteous people to lure them away from trusting God. The Holy Spirit is guiding us out of tests, not putting us through trials. The trying of Job's faith was not initiated by God. Satan was trying to find a way to turn him against God. What Job faced was evil, not holy, just like sickness is evil.

> *"An evil disease," they say, "clings to him. And now that he lies down, he will rise up no more."*
>
> Psalms 41:8

"Evil disease," in this verse, is also translated as "a thing of Belial." Sickness is evil; it's from the devil. God doesn't use the work of the devil to teach us. Yes, we go through tests and trials, but God doesn't enlist the devil's assistance to teach us. So why did Job go through what he went through? Job was a righteous man, but he was afraid and that fear opened the door for the devil to attack him.

> *For the thing I greatly feared has come upon me, and what I dreaded has happened to me.*
>
> Job 3:25

The answer to fear is knowing that God loves you.

> *And we have known and believed the love that God has for us. God is love, and he who abides in love abides in God, and God in him. Love has been perfected among us in this: that we may have boldness in the day of judgment; because as He is, so are we in this world. There is no fear in love; but perfect love casts out fear, because fear involves torment. But he who fears has not been made perfect in love. We love Him because He first loved us.*
>
> 1 John 4:16-19

Knowing the love God has for you drives away all fear and gives you the courage to face anything the devil throws at you.

There are different ways he will test your faith. He will challenge God's Word by asking, "Did God really mean that?" He will question God's character, "Will He keep His promises for you?" He will get you to look at the natural, "It's obvious you're not healed; you're still in pain." And then he will make you think it will never happen, "It's been months and you're still not healed."

Job is not our example of how to go through a test. Jesus demonstrated how to deal with the devil during a trial. When the devil tested Him in the desert, Jesus responded by saying, "It is written!" (Matthew 4:1-11). God's truths will always get you the victory. The devil is a thief. He is the one trying to steal what belongs to you. You aren't the sick trying to get well, you are the healed and the devil is trying to steal it. God doesn't test us with sickness. The devil makes people sick and then blames God.

Chapter 6

Hindrance # 4

Some say,
"My suffering will bring God glory."

The LORD existed before man. He is the "All-Sufficient One." He has been the all-in-all since before time. Our experiences do not make Him greater or lesser. He does not need to perform miracles in our lives to prove that He is our creator. It doesn't give Him a boost every time we receive healing, and He doesn't heal just for people to recognize Him as God.

As a Father, He loves to see us get healed; that's always His desire. People may see the miracle and praise Him, but that doesn't mean He was waiting to heal them until He would get the glory. Letting people remain sick is not love. God wants all of mankind to know that He loves them and wants to see them healed right now.

When it comes to God getting glory for healings, the following passage can be misunderstood.

> *Now as Jesus passed by, He saw a man who was blind from birth. And His disciples asked Him, saying, "Rabbi, who sinned, this man or his parents, that he was born blind?" Jesus answered, "Neither this man nor his parents sinned, but that the works of God should be revealed in him.*
> *John 9:1-3*

Take a look at it in the Contemporary English Version.

> As Jesus walked along, he saw a man who had been
> blind since birth. Jesus' disciples asked, "Teacher, why
> was this man born blind? Was it because he or his
> parents sinned?"   "No, it wasn't!" Jesus answered. "But
> because of his blindness, you will see God work a
> miracle for him.
>
> John 9:1-3 CEV

God didn't make the man sick so that He could heal him one
day. That would be a cruel master, not a loving Father. Jesus
healed him because He had compassion on Him, not because He
wanted to get glory. He was often "moved with compassion" for
the sick.

> And when Jesus went out He saw a great multitude; and
> He was moved with compassion for them, and healed
> their sick.
>
> Matthew 14:14

> So Jesus had compassion and touched their eyes. And
> immediately their eyes received sight, and they followed
> Him.
>
> Matthew 20:34

> Then Jesus, moved with compassion, stretched out His
> hand and touched him, and said to him, "I am willing; be
> cleansed."
>
> Mark 1:41

Jesus didn't heal because He wanted worship or recognition as
the Son of God; He healed because of His love for the people.
He hated to see them sick. A man once asked me, "Why do you
pray for the sick so much?" I answered, "Because I love them. I
don't want to see them sick." God is not keeping people from

getting healed so that others will give Him praise when they receive healing. He is love (1 John 4:8) and love would never make someone sick in order to get glory later when He made them well.

Christians suffer for the Kingdom of God. Many were killed in the early ages of the church. The Bible promises there will be persecution (2 Timothy 3:12), but sickness is not part of it. Paul was shipwrecked, beaten, and stoned until he almost died, but he never mentions sickness as one of the things he suffered. His "thorn-in-the-flesh" was a messenger of Satan sent to hinder everything he did; it was not a physical ailment (2 Corinthians 11:23 - 12:10). God gave Paul a revelation of how to operate in His grace in order to be victorious, not how to suffer. God does not use sickness or disease to prove our sincerity or commitment to Him; He always heals.

And He said to me, "My grace is sufficient for you, for My strength is made perfect in weakness." Therefore most gladly I will rather boast in my infirmities, that the power of Christ may rest upon me. Therefore I take pleasure in infirmities, in reproaches, in needs, in persecutions, in distresses, for Christ's sake. For when I am weak, then I am strong.
2 Corinthians 12:9-10

The word "infirmity" can be used to describe physical sickness; it means to be feeble and weak. It is also the translation for spiritual inability. Paul uses "infirmity" here to describe his lack of strength when attacked by the "messenger of Satan". Paul was requesting God's help to be victorious in a spiritual battle, not physical sickness. The answer to his prayer came when he got a revelation of God's power and ability within him to overcome any attack of the enemy. He realized that authority and power come from the Holy Spirit within, not from his

23

natural ability. This revelation gave him the confidence to "boast" about God's strength and not his own.

Some people find themselves desperate for a miracle and promise God that they will do something that brings Him glory if He heals them. They may say, *"God, if you heal me I will serve you for the rest of my life."* God doesn't need a reason to heal you. Jesus already went to the cross and gave you healing. Your promise is not the reason He is going to heal you. If you think God is waiting until you do something before He heals you, it will keep you from receiving healing. He is not withholding healing; He is waiting for you to receive what He has already done.

Chapter 7

Hindrance # 5

Some say,
"You have a generational curse."

Deuteronomy 28 states that if you obey God's laws you will be blessed; if you do not obey the laws, you will be cursed. It goes on to describe all the curses that will come upon you. All kinds of sickness and disease are mentioned. Then in verse 61 it says, *"Every sickness and every plague, which is not written in this Book of the Law, will the LORD bring upon you until you are destroyed."* It is very clear, under the Law; you have to keep the commands of the Law in order to be healed.

God made a covenant through Moses; it was the Law. God's commandments guaranteed that you would be blessed if you obeyed them, but no one was able to keep the Law. God knew that was going to happen, so before Adam was created, it was ordained that Jesus would be our substitute (Revelation 13:8); He would fulfill our responsibility to the covenant. A covenant requires it to be enforced until one of the partners dies. By taking our place, Jesus brought to an end the requirement to keep the Law in order to receive God's blessing. He died so that we could receive healing apart from the Law.

Because finding fault with them, He says: "Behold, the days are coming, says the Lord, when I will make a new covenant with the house of Israel and with the house of Judah: according to the covenant that I made with their fathers in the day that I took them by the hand to lead the out of the land of Egypt; because they did not continue in My covenant, and I disregarded them, says the Lord. For this is the covenant that I will make with the house of Israel after those days, says the Lord: I will put my laws in their mind and write them on their hearts; and I will be their God, and they shall be My people. None of them shall teach his neighbor, and none his brother, saying, 'Know the Lord,' for all shall know Me, from the least of them to the greatest of them. For I will be merciful to their unrighteousness, and their sins and their lawless deeds I will remember no more." In that He says, "A new covenant," He has made the first obsolete. Now what is becoming obsolete and growing old is ready to vanish away.

Hebrews 8:8-13

We are no longer under the Covenant of the Law. Jesus fulfilled every requirement. All of our past, present, and future sins are covered by the Blood of Jesus (Colossians 2:13-14). This doesn't mean we want to sin; it means we no longer have to prove we are deserving of God's love. All of the curses that came from disobedience have now been abolished and we get to enjoy the promises of God, including healing.

Christ has redeemed us from the curse of the law, having become a curse for us (for it is written, "Cursed is everyone who hangs on a tree"), that the blessing of Abraham might come upon the Gentiles in Christ Jesus, that we might receive the promise of the Spirit through faith.

Galatians 3:13-14

We have been redeemed from all the curses mentioned in Deuteronomy 28. If you see a curse mentioned in that chapter, then you know you are redeemed from it. But what if it is a curse that has been passed down through your family?

Generational curses are mentioned in this passage in Exodus:

> *And the LORD passed before him and proclaimed, "The LORD, the LORD God, merciful and gracious, longsuffering, and abounding in goodness and truth, keeping mercy for thousands, forgiving iniquity and transgression and sin, by no means clearing the guilty, visiting the iniquity of the fathers upon the children and the children's children to the third and the fourth generation."*
>
> *Exodus 34:6-7*

Under the Law, the children of the guilty would be cursed; but God spoke through Ezekiel these words:

> *"What do you mean when you use this proverb concerning the land of Israel, saying: 'The fathers have eaten sour grapes, and the children's teeth are set on edge'?" "As I live," says the Lord GOD, "You shall no longer use this proverb in Israel. "Behold, all souls are Mine; the soul of the father as well as the soul of the son is Mine; the soul who sins shall die."*
>
> *Ezekiel 18:2-4*

The one who sins is the one who is punished. God isn't going to curse you for something your grandfather did. When you were born again, you became a part of God's family. You have a new blood line. Even if your family has genetic conditions, you are redeemed from every sickness and disease. The Law required obedience in order to avoid curses; Jesus met the requirements of the Law for us and now we are free from every curse, including generational curses.

Chapter 8

Hindrance # 6

Some say,
"You have sin in your life."

Sin does not stop God from healing you. Obviously, sin is a horrible thing. It invites fear and guilt into your thoughts and causes you to withdraw from God, but God doesn't heal people because they deserve it. He heals people because He loves them and Jesus has already paid the price for sickness.

> *Who Himself bore our sins in His own body on the tree,*
> *that we, having died to sins, might live for*
> *righteousness—by whose stripes you were healed.*
> *1 Peter 2:24*

This verse says we were healed because Jesus bore our sin and took stripes on His back. Why did Jesus have to be punished in order to heal us? Sickness is the beginning stages of death. Death was introduced into the world when Adam and Eve sinned.

> *Therefore, just as through one man sin entered the*
> *world, and death through sin, and thus death spread to*
> *all men, because all sinned.*
> *Romans 5:12*

Stripes were the punishment for sin in the Old Testament. Jesus paid the price for all of mankind's sin by taking stripes on His back.

> *For if by the one man's offense death reigned through the one, much more those who receive abundance of grace and of the gift of righteousness will reign in life through the One, Jesus Christ. Therefore, as through one man's offense judgment came to all men, resulting in condemnation, even so through one Man's righteous act the free gift came to all men, resulting in justification of life. For as by one man's disobedience many were made sinners, so also by one Man's obedience many will be made righteous.*
>
> *Romans 5:17-19*

Since sin has now been paid for, everything that was the result of sin is also paid for. Sickness is one of the byproducts of sin. It is a path to death and came with sin. Jesus died for sin, eliminating everything it caused. Now we don't have to pay for sin and we don't have to be sick.

> *For He made Him who knew no sin to be sin for us, that we might become the righteousness of God in Him.*
>
> *2 Corinthians 5:21*

We become righteous when we accept Jesus as our savior. He removes our sin nature and makes us brand new.

> *Therefore, if anyone is in Christ, he is a new creation; old things have passed away; behold, all things have become new.*
>
> *2 Corinthians 5:17*

"Brand new" means something that never existed before. We are not the old man put back together. He made us righteous and gave us His life.

> *For God so loved the world that He gave His only begotten Son, that whoever believes in Him should not perish but have everlasting life.*
>
> *John 3:16*

God made us righteous so that we could be with Him. Sin separated us, Jesus restored us. Now that we are righteous, the Holy Spirit can dwell in us. Having the Holy Spirit in us brings life to our bodies.

> *But if the Spirit of Him who raised Jesus from the dead dwells in you, He who raised Christ from the dead will also give life to your mortal bodies through His Spirit who dwells in you.*
>
> *Romans 8:11*

You no longer have sin and death living in you. You are righteous and the life of God is in you. You let this life work in you by acting like you are righteous. Peter said to, *"Live for righteousness,"* in 1 Peter 2:24. The devil will try to stop you from living in that righteousness by reminding you of your sin, but there is good news:

> *There is therefore now no condemnation to those who are in Christ Jesus, who do not walk according to the flesh, but according to the Spirit.*
>
> *Romans 8:1*

Sin-consciousness will keep you sick. You have to reject those thoughts and live by the power of the Holy Spirit in you. God dealt with sin. You have been made righteous. You can live free from condemnation by saying, "I am forgiven. I have been made righteous by the Blood of Jesus. I refuse to think otherwise." Even if you sinned this morning, it is covered by the Blood of Jesus. Repent, stop seeing yourself as a sinner, and receive your healing as a child of God.

Chapter 9

Hindrance # 7

Some say,
"It's your own fault."

A friend of mine was skiing and hurt his knee. He sat in a chair later that night with his leg all wrapped up and asked the Father a simple question, "God, do you heal idiots?" How many things have we done to ourselves that need God's intervention? Bad diets, no exercise, extreme sports, smoking, drugs, accidents, or maybe even slipping on the ice; all of these could be called our fault, but we still need healing, so you have to ask the question: "Can a person neglect or abuse their body and expect God to heal them?"

God's natural laws are just as divine as His spiritual laws; but they are not greater. The reason people have a hard time receiving healing for things that they caused is they believe the natural laws are greater. They believe that if the cause came by natural means, then the answer, if there is one, has to come from the natural. But this scripture says the natural originates from the spirit realm.

By faith we understand that the worlds were framed by the word of God, so that the things which are seen were not made of things which are visible.

Hebrews 11:3

Even though the sickness or injury was caused by your poor choices, God is still able to supernaturally reverse what you have done and heal your body. You do not have to suffer the consequences of your choices; Jesus has already suffered for you.

> *He sent His word and healed them, and delivered them from their destructions.*
>
> Psalms 107:20

This verse implies that God delivered them from the pit they dug for themselves. It doesn't matter how you got into the mess you are in, Jesus has already bought your healing. He knew you would make bad choices, and He took the consequences of those choices on His back so that you can be healed of every disease, sickness and injury. Here is an example of an injury being healed:

> *When those around Him saw what was going to happen, they said to Him, "Lord, shall we strike with the sword?" And one of them struck the servant of the high priest and cut off his right ear. But Jesus answered and said, "Permit even this." And He touched his ear and healed him.*
>
> Luke 22:49-51

Malchus, the servant of the high priest, was in the garden to arrest Jesus. He was merely doing his job. Peter drew his sword and swung it at Malchus cutting off his ear. It's a good thing he ducked; otherwise he might have cut off his head! Malchus was not sick and didn't have a disease; he was injured by Peter's sword. Jesus immediately stopped the fight and healed his ear; proving that injuries can be healed instantly.

Whether it is your fault or someone else's; it doesn't mean you should ignore the leading of the Holy Spirit and abuse your body. The Holy Spirit knows what we need to do in order for our bodies to function properly. If we listen, He will guide us around the enemy's snares and into a life of health. It is impossible to operate in faith and ignore God's directions. You are the temple where God has chosen to dwell. Letting flesh rule and allowing your body to be in poor condition will not change His love for you, but it is better to respond to His promptings and care for your body.

We are never to be performance minded when it comes to healing; but we shouldn't be lazy, carnal, and uncaring either. The devil uses our weaknesses to keep us bound and unable to do what God has planned for our lives. Changing your diet or starting to exercise is not the source of healing. Healing comes when you believe that Jesus bore your sickness and carried your pain. But remember, ignoring the guidance of the Holy Spirit will leave the door open for the devil to attack again.

When I was twenty-nine years old, I got a severe kidney infection and ended up in the hospital for thirty-six hours. The doctors gave me antibiotics and the infection left. Someone had told me, "If you know what it is and where it came from, you can resist it." But I didn't know what caused the infection and I ended up in the hospital. I asked God why I couldn't get my healing. He told me, "It doesn't matter what it is or where it came from, it doesn't belong in your body." I was trying to fix whatever caused the infection, but I couldn't figure it out. God showed me that I can resist all sickness; even if I don't know what it is. After that, I stopped looking for the cause and began to focus on receiving healing.

You can be healed even if the sickness was your fault. You didn't earn your salvation, and you are never going to earn your healing. Healing is a gift of God's mercy. We receive it by humbly accepting what He has done. You can't make changes to your lifestyle and expect God to heal you because of your performance. He has already healed you; you make changes because you value His guidance.

Chapter 10

Hindrance # 8

Some say,
"You haven't done enough to be healed."

What is the biggest hindrance to faith? Works, trying to earn what God has given as a gift. Healing is a gift. You can't earn it. The devil will tell you that you haven't done enough to deserve healing. We can never do enough. The only way we can receive healing from God, is if He gives it to us by grace.

> *For by grace you have been saved through faith, and that not of yourselves; it is the gift of God, not of works, lest anyone should boast.*
>
> *Ephesians 2:8-9*

The Greek word translated "saved" is "*sozo*," and it also means to be healed (Mark 5:23 and Acts 14:9). We are saved and healed by grace. It's a gift. We receive the gift of healing by faith. It isn't by earning it. If we were able to earn it, we could tell everyone what we did to get it. Jesus took sickness for us and gave us health; we didn't do anything. He has already done everything necessary in order for us to be healed. We can't add to it.

It's human nature to want to do something to get healed. If we don't see a change in our body immediately, we begin trying to get healed. Some people take medicine, change their diet, or stop bad habits in order to get healed; however, healing is available to you apart from what you do. The changes you make should be based on the leading of the Holy Spirit, not in order to get your healing. If you feel compelled to earn healing or at least do your part, you are on the "performance plan," not the grace plan. God does not ask us to do anything before He heals us. He asks us to make changes because He has healed us.

There are a number of reasons why people try to earn healing. Some try to get God's approval or to prove that they are worthy of being healed. Others desire to do their part so that they feel like they are part of the solution. And others feel guilty and want to make things right, but God chose to love you before you ever did anything to deserve that love. Your actions are not going to change how He feels about you. How you perform as a Christian does not determine whether God will heal you. He heals you because He loves you.

> But God demonstrates His own love toward us, in that while we were still sinners, Christ died for us.
>
> *Romans 5:8*

As humans, we like the feelings of success. We want to feel like we earned what we have. There is a sense of accomplishment when we do a good job and earn pay; we can congratulate ourselves and show off what we have accomplished—but it takes humility to receive a gift.

> But He gives more grace. Therefore He says: "God resists the proud, but gives grace to the humble."
>
> *James 4:6*

Pride stops the flow of grace. To be "graced" with something means it is a gift. You didn't earn it; you didn't deserve it. Everything we receive by faith comes as grace, a gift. In fact, God chose faith as the way we receive from Him so that He can give us everything as a gift (grace).

Therefore it is of faith that it might be according to grace, so that the promise might be sure to all the seed, not only to those who are of the law, but also to those who are of the faith of Abraham, who is the father of us all.

Romans 4:16

God knew we couldn't earn healing, so He gave it to us. In order to make it available to all, apart from earning or deserving it, He made grace for healing available by faith. All we have to do to receive the gift of healing is say, "Thank you," and receive it.

Through whom also we have access by faith into this grace in which we stand, and rejoice in hope of the glory of God.

Romans 5:2

Receiving a gift can be humbling. If you are given a gift from the heart, it is easy to feel like you don't deserve the gift. If the present is huge and expensive, you may feel intimidated and unworthy. Homemade gifts that were made with love can also overwhelm you. You feel like there is no way to return the gesture.

God knows you didn't earn healing and may not deserve it. Even though you may be sick because of something you did, God chose to make healing a gift so that everyone can have it. If you feel guilty and think you deserve to be sick, do not try to earn healing; and when you receive the gift of healing, don't try to pay Him back. God forgives the worst sin, and He also heals anything that you brought upon yourself.

Chapter 11

Hindrance # 9

Some say,
"You just don't have enough faith."

People say, "You don't have enough faith to be healed"; as if everything depended on you. Yes, we receive healing by faith, but not faith in our ability; it's faith in Jesus. Jesus is the healer, not you. Faith is confidence in Him.

> *[Abraham], being fully convinced that what He had promised He was also able to perform.*
>
> *Romans 4:21*

Abraham was the father of faith. He believed when it seemed impossible. He was so convinced that he never wavered. Now that's confidence! But where did he place his confidence? It was in God. It wasn't in his ability to believe; he had confidence in his covenant partner, God. If God said it, He would do it.

We don't have faith in a process; we have faith in a person. Let me give you an illustration:

> If I ask my friend to pick me up at the airport and take me home, should I worry if he is late? My friend is reliable, trustworthy, and good for his word, so I know I shouldn't worry. There is a process required in order to get to the airport and there are lots of things that could keep my friend from arriving on time. He could be

delayed by someone at home, He could be stuck in traffic, or maybe his car had a flat tire. All of these could be why the process of picking me up was delayed. But my faith is not in the natural circumstances, it is in him. Because I know him, I trust him, and I know he will come.

The more we know God, the more confidence we will have in Him. The more we read and understand His Word, the better we will know His will. When we are convinced that God always keeps His Word, we will act in faith even though it looks impossible. Jesus said to have faith in God. He is reliable, trustworthy, and He always keeps His word.

So Jesus answered and said to them, "Have faith in God."

Mark 11:22

I remember when I believed God for something and it was taking a long time to receive it. Years passed, and I still didn't have it. While in prayer one day, I asked God what was taking so long. He asked me, "What does My Word say?" I quoted three scriptures that promised me I could have it. He responded, "That's all you need to know." At that very moment I knew that God always keeps His Word and the promise was on the way. A few months later, I had it.

Faith is like the little swirly circle on the computer when you are waiting for a site to load. You clicked on the link, but nothing changed. All you can see is the circle spinning on the page, but that little swirl is all you need to know that the page is coming. You can't see it. There haven't been any changes, but you know it is coming. Just because you can't see any changes yet doesn't mean God isn't working on it. Don't focus on the process; there could be lots of things that cause delay. Have faith in Him.

How do you feel after reading about these hindrances? Do you sense a difference? Do you feel lighter on the inside? Religion's way of thinking is so burdensome. It makes you feel heavy with everything that is required of you. Healing is not something we need to work for. Jesus already did all the work. We need to learn how to rest and receive.

Chapter 12

Revelation is the Key

Faith is like a fruit. It grows naturally as you meditate on the Word; it is not something we force into existence or demand to happen. You receive faith the instant you get revelation.

> *So then faith comes by hearing, and hearing by the word of God.*
>
> Romans 10:17

"Word", in this verse, is translated from the Greek word *"rhema."* This word means "a spoken word," not just something you read. It's a specific word from God for your current situation. It's alive; straight from the Spirit of God. You can't have faith without this *rhema*.

Rhema also means the revealing of God's will. It's a revelation of how God sees your situation. If we could see what God sees, it would change our entire way of thinking. When you have revelation, you go from fear and worry to excitement and confidence.

> *Faith is the confidence that what we hope for will actually happen; it gives us assurance about things we cannot see.*
>
> Hebrews 11:1 NLT

Our confidence does not come from our ability but from knowing what God knows. *Rhema* is when God reveals His plan to us. It happens in an instant; it's as if we see something we have never seen before. God gives us an instantaneous download of His knowledge. In the blink of an eye, we see what God sees. No longer are we weighed down by the burden of trying to get a solution, we know the entire plan. We can see the outcome even though it hasn't happened yet.

Revelation is the key to faith. A car can't run without the key. You can't unlock a door without a key. You can't solve a puzzle without the key. We have to have a revelation in order to be in faith. We have to know what God knows.

Many people desiring healing sincerely believe that God wants them to be healed but haven't heard from God, specifically, regarding their situation. They have heard that God heals, but they don't know if God is going to heal them. Because they still have the symptoms of sickness, they assume they have not been healed. What you see or feel does not determine what God has done. A person in faith rests in the Word received from God; they don't continue trying to get healing, because they have already heard from God and received healing by faith.

Chapter 13

Faith Doesn't Look at the Natural

Faith doesn't labor for the things of God. It receives what has already been done. Jesus took stripes on His back so that we can be healthy. This happened 2,000 years ago. He took your place for every disease. The work is finished, and everything you need in order to be healed has already been provided. All you have to do is plug into the healing power and receive.

> *Who Himself bore our sins in His own body on the tree, that we, having died to sins, might live for righteousness—by whose stripes you were healed.*
> *1 Peter 2:24*

This verse says you "were healed"; not that you are "going to be healed." You already are healed. You may ask, "How can this be? I still feel the symptoms in my body." Faith does not look at what it sees; it looks at what God sees.

> *While we do not look at the things which are seen, but at the things which are not seen. For the things which are seen are temporary, but the things which are not seen are eternal.*
> *2 Corinthians 4:18*

Just because you can see it does not mean it can't change. If it came, it can leave. The things of the natural are changeable; they are temporary. The plan of God is eternal; it overrides anything happening in the natural. Life and health are greater than death and sickness. We need to take our focus off what we see in the natural and fix our attention on what God sees in the spirit.

For we walk by faith, not by sight.

2 Corinthians 5:7

Your mind and body will try to convince you that what you see and feel is permanent or unchangeable. The only way to know that your symptoms are temporary is for God to reveal His will to you. Faith is being convinced that the symptoms are leaving. It is a confidence that rises out of your spirit because you have heard from God (*rhema*). This kind of revelation produces faith. It enables you to believe God's Word no matter what you see or feel. The only way to get faith is by revelation. Focus on hearing from God regarding your situation in order to get faith. Once you hear from God, you will be in faith and have the confidence to not go by what you see.

Chapter 14

Look to Jesus

Jesus is the answer to our problems because He provided healing for us, so the best way to receive healing is to take your eyes off the sickness and put your focus on Jesus. Jesus demonstrated this when He went to raise Lazarus from the dead.

When He arrived in Bethany, everyone was crying and upset that He hadn't come sooner. They were all focused on what they could see, but they didn't know what Jesus knew; He had heard from the Father that Lazarus would live. To get them into the realm of faith He had to get their attention off the natural events and onto God. To do this, He began to pray out loud so everyone could hear.

> *Then they took away the stone from the place where the dead man was lying. And Jesus lifted up His eyes and said, "Father, I thank You that You have heard Me. And I know that You always hear Me, but because of the people who are standing by I said this, that they may believe that You sent Me."*
>
> *John 11:41-42*

He turned all of their eyes to the Father; that's where healing comes from. It doesn't come from the minister who's praying. As long as their eyes were focused on the natural, on what they could see, nothing was going to change. By changing their focus, He made a way for them to receive. When all of their eyes were on the Father, Jesus commanded Lazarus to come back to life, and he walked out of the grave.

It's easy to see nothing but the symptoms. They are constantly trying to draw attention to themselves. If you are in severe pain, it's difficult to think about anything else, but instead of looking to see if the sickness has left, focus on the Healer. Once you receive healing, the symptoms will leave.

Chapter 15

How do I Receive Healing?

What does it mean to receive healing? It's kind of like receiving a gift. If someone hands you a gift, all you have to do is reach out and take it. That's the easiest part. The part that is unseen is the person earning money, going to the store, buying the gift, wrapping it up with a big bow, and driving it to your house. They do all the work, and you just say, "Thank you." God sent Jesus. He suffered and died. He wrapped healing with a huge bow and is lovingly holding the gift out to you. Now all you have to do is take it and say, "Thank you."

> *Therefore I say to you, whatever things you ask when you pray, believe that you receive them, and you will have them.*
>
> *Mark 11:24*

The original Greek word for "receive" means "to take." You can't receive something unless you take it. You have to reach out and claim it. This is often done by just acting in faith. Now, keep in mind, in order to act in faith, you have to first hear from God. But once you have heard, it changes your thinking, your acting, and what you are saying. Take a look at these stories:

> *Then as He entered a certain village, there met Him ten men who were lepers, who stood afar off. And they lifted up their voices and said, "Jesus, Master, have mercy on us!" So when He saw them, He said to them,*

"Go, show yourselves to the priests." And so it was that as they went, they were cleansed.

Luke 17:12-14

They had no signs of healing after Jesus ministered to them; they still looked sick, but by acting on the word of Jesus, they were healed. There is no way a leper would have started walking to the priest without a word from God. That *rhema* gave them the faith they needed to believe that they were healed and the symptoms would leave. That word changed the way they acted.

Then He said to the man, "Stretch out your hand." And he stretched it out, and it was restored as whole as the other.

Matthew 12:13

That was impossible. His hand had been withered for years. How was he supposed to stretch it out? But Jesus said to do it. That was all he had to hear. It took faith to lift his arm and reach out like his hand was normal. It hadn't been normal in a long time; why even bother to lift it? It was the spoken word from Jesus that sparked confidence in him. Those words inspired him to do what he hadn't done for a long while. Without even thinking, he reached out, and as he did, the hand was restored.

And in Lystra a certain man without strength in his feet was sitting, a cripple from his mother's womb, who had never walked. This man heard Paul speaking. Paul, observing him intently and seeing that he had faith to be healed, said with a loud voice, "Stand up straight on your feet!" And he leaped and walked.

Acts 14:8-10

Hearing the gospel from Paul gave this man faith. Every word Paul spoke was alive. His words contained power. The Holy

Spirit was moving inside the crippled man as he sat and listened. Paul could see that the man was being changed on the inside. He could see that the man had faith. He must have been squirming with anticipation. All he needed was a spark to set him off. Then suddenly, Paul shouted, "Stand up!" That's all it took. He just needed to know what to do with all this pent-up excitement. The man leaped to his feet and walked for the first time.

It was more than head knowledge after hearing a good speech. The Spirit-inspired words about Jesus gave this man faith, and the words were alive inside him. He didn't leap to his feet because he wanted to; he had wanted to walk for his entire life. He leaped because, now, he knew he could.

Faith is not a well-calculated plan. It doesn't make sense. All the natural circumstances say you can't. Faith is a fire inside that can't be put out. It is waiting for the moment it will burst out of its container and show everyone what God has done. This kind of internal excitement and confidence only comes from having heard from God. Until you actually hear God's plan, you should listen to the Word. Meditate, confess, declare, and act like God's Word is true. Once you have heard from God and receive faith, your thoughts, words, and actions become alive. You become convinced that God has already done the miracle and begin acting like you have it; expecting it to manifest.

Chapter 16

You Already are Healed

Many people are waiting to see changes in their bodies before they believe they are healed. People that are in faith believe they are already healed, even if none of the symptoms have changed. According to Mark 11:24, you have to believe that you have received healing before you actually see it manifest. You have to believe that the gift has already been purchased, wrapped, and is on the way, before it ever gets to you.

1 Peter 2:24 says, *"By His stripes you were healed."* You aren't going to be healed; you were healed. Jesus has already healed you. You might ask, "How can that be possible? If He already healed me, then why am I sick?" Those are great questions. Let's compare it to salvation.

Jesus died just once, for all of mankind (Romans 6:10). Anyone who declares Jesus as their Lord and accepts Him as their Savior is a new creature in Christ; they are born again. But there are millions that aren't born-again. Does that mean Jesus hasn't saved them? No, it means they haven't accepted that Christ died in their stead. As soon as they do, they are made righteous. Just because there are people that haven't been saved yet, it doesn't mean that Christ hasn't already died for them. In the same manner, many still don't know that Jesus already took their place for all sickness, disease, and injuries. As soon as they hear about it, and accept it, they can be healed.

God can't do what He has already done and He can't give you what He has already given you. Jesus has already healed you; all you have to do is believe and accept it. It's really that easy. It gets complicated when we try to earn what already belongs to us. It's human nature to want to fix what we mess up or create a way to get God's blessing. You don't have to do anything. Rest! Jesus did all the work and He's offering you a gift. Take it and say, "Thank you."

Chapter 17

You Can Receive Healing Today

People are oftentimes looking for someone to pray for them so they can receive healing. They send messages by social media, they start prayer chains, or they go to the pastor and ask him to pray. You don't have to do any of that. You can receive from God yourself. You don't have to wait.

The first step is to set your mind on Jesus. It's not about having the right music or a quiet place. You can focus your heart on the Lord anywhere, anytime, even in a crowded, noisy shopping center. Just start thinking about Jesus and how He took your place on the cross. Allow your mind to imagine Him dying for you. The presence of God will become noticeable. You will be able to tell by the peace in your heart and calmness in your mind.

Once you have your focus on Jesus, ask Him about His plan for your current situation, then wait until you hear from Him. If you are wondering what God's voice sounds like, do this: close your eyes and think your name to yourself. Just say it in your head. That is the same voice that God uses to speak to you. It comes out of your heart. Oftentimes it's like carrying on a conversation inside your head, but it is wiser than you usually think or smarter than your normal ideas. He will give you thoughts that are beyond you; it's obvious that you didn't come up with it.

It isn't always a conversation, sometimes it's an impression or an image. You have an idea come to you, or you see yourself doing something. God will speak in plain language and also in imagery. If you don't understand what He is saying, ask Him about it. Sometimes, He will take you an unexpected route in order to get you where you need to be. I'll explain.

I came home from overseas and found myself going to the bathroom a lot. I knew I had eaten something that messed me up. I don't know what it was or how I got it, but I knew to take it seriously. I asked God what I should do, "Should I go to the doctor or the pharmacy to get medicine or should I trust you to heal me and wait?" Within seconds of asking the question, my mind drifted and I began thinking about something totally different. I found myself contemplating all the reasons why you should tithe. That sounds crazy. I was totally off topic.

My thoughts finally concluded that tithing comes down to covenant. I have a covenant with God. As soon as I thought "covenant," the bells in my head went off. The light came on. I had a revelation from God. Instantly, I knew angels were fighting on my behalf because of the covenant I have with God. If I was sick, then He was going to take care of it as if He was sick. I didn't have to worry about it; I would be well.

A few days later, there were no more symptoms. Yes, the symptoms took a couple days to leave, but that's not when I was healed. I was healed 2,000 years ago, and I received it when I got the revelation. The concern I had left as soon as I heard from God. I didn't go to the doctor or buy any medicine; I knew everything would be okay.

Chapter 18

Act on God's Word to You

After you have heard from God, all you have to do is act on it. However, I want to caution you—don't act unless you have heard from God. God doesn't require you to do something in order to be healed. You act because you have heard from Him and believe you are already healed. You don't have to fast and pray to prove your worthiness. Fasting changes you, it doesn't change God. It will cause your flesh to be submitted, but it doesn't make God more willing to heal you. And don't throw away your medicine to show God, or anyone else, that you believe. That doesn't produce faith or get God's attention. You should only act after you have a revelation that God has already healed you, not to get God to heal you.

Sometimes people want to be in faith so they do something they saw others do; or they act out what they would do if they were healed. This can be dangerous or a hindrance to your faith if you haven't heard from God. God doesn't require action to get faith. Action is a response to the faith you have. Now, there are times when God will direct you to change what you are doing in order to remain healed, but what you need to do is not the prerequisite to receiving healing. This story from the Pool of Bethesda will illustrate what I mean:

> *Now a certain man was there who had an infirmity thirty-eight years. When Jesus saw him lying there, and knew that he already had been in that condition a long time, He said to him, "Do you want to be made well?" The sick man answered Him, "Sir, I have no man to put*

me into the pool when the water is stirred up; but while I am coming, another steps down before me." Jesus said to him, "Rise, take up your bed and walk." And immediately the man was made well, took up his bed, and walked. And that day was the Sabbath. The Jews therefore said to him who was cured, "It is the Sabbath; it is not lawful for you to carry your bed." He answered them, "He who made me well said to me, 'Take up your bed and walk.'" Then they asked him, "Who is the Man who said to you, 'Take up your bed and walk'?" But the one who was healed did not know who it was, for Jesus had withdrawn, a multitude being in that place. Afterward Jesus found him in the temple, and said to him, "See, you have been made well. Sin no more, lest a worse thing come upon you."

John 5:5-14

Jesus asked the man if he wanted to be healed. He didn't ask the man if he wanted to be forgiven, but He did indicate that the man's sin opened the door for his suffering. The man was not required to repent or make amends for his sins in order to be healed. Now, don't be afraid that you may have an open door; if God shows you something, deal with it. Jesus never looked at a person's past to figure out how to heal them. In regards to this man, Jesus came to him later and told him not to sin any more so that he could keep the door closed to the devil.

Chapter 19

Have a Listening Heart

I remember having a sore back for a while. I asked the Lord what I should do and He said, "Sit up when you ride in the truck." You see, I was riding several hours a day in our truck. My dad would drive to the jobsite, and I would slouch down in the seat and try to sleep on the way to the job. Apparently, my back was being twisted more than it should. I began to sit up on our drive and the back pain left. I know that God cares about every area of my life, even my back pain. His wisdom saved me from being in pain every day. God has wisdom for every area of our lives. If we will ask, He will give us direction.

> *If any of you lacks wisdom, let him ask of God, who gives to all liberally and without reproach, and it will be given to him. But let him ask in faith, with no doubting, for he who doubts is like a wave of the sea driven and tossed by the wind. For let not that man suppose that he will receive anything from the Lord; he is a double-minded man, unstable in all his ways.*
>
> *James 1:5-8*

God never withholds His wisdom from us; if we ask in faith, we will get an answer. So how do we ask in faith? Faith believes everything God says, without any hesitation. Doubt comes when you have second thoughts. If you are tossed between God's Word and what you are experiencing, you are in doubt; your heart says God has healed you, but your body says you are still sick. When your mind can't figure out which one to believe, you are double-minded. Being in doubt means you aren't convinced that God's Word is superior to what you feel or see. By purposing to listen to God's Word, you will become convinced that His promises are true. Faith comes once you receive revelation of the truth.

> *If you are willing and obedient, you shall eat the good of the land;*
>
> *Isaiah 1:19*

The original Hebrew word for "obedient" in this verse is also translated as "a listening heart." Having a listening heart is the key to becoming single-minded. But it isn't just about listening; you have to have a desire to put into practice the things God shows you. The best way to approach God is to say, "Father, you have the wisdom that I need. Reveal your wisdom to me and help me put it into practice." Coming to God instead of waiting for Him to do something, shows a willingness to apply what He says. If you will be proactive and willing to do whatever He says, you will receive wisdom regarding healing.

I never did like the word "obedient." It always made me feel like a soldier saying, "Yes, Sir!" to a commanding officer. We have a relationship with God; we aren't His slaves, we are His sons and daughters. But if we don't follow His direction, we will miss out on what He is giving us.

> *Jesus answered and said to him, "If anyone loves Me, he will keep My word; and My Father will love him, and We will come to him and make Our home with him. He who does not love Me does not keep My words; and the word which you hear is not Mine but the Father's who sent Me."*
>
> *John 14:23-24*

Some people may think that their obedience is proof that they love God, but that isn't how it works. We keep His commands from the love that we have for Him; not to prove our love. Our love is a response to the love that He has shown us.

We love Him because He first loved us.

1 John 4:19

The Passion Translation shows that it is His love for us that gives us the power to do what He has asked.

Jesus replied, "Loving me empowers you to obey my word. And my Father will love you so deeply that we will come to you and make you our dwelling place. But those who don't love me will not obey my words. The Father did not send me to speak my own revelation, but the words of my Father."

John 14:23-24 TPT

When you know that God loves you, it is easy to do what He says. If you focus on your ability to obey, you will become frustrated. You can never perform well enough to earn God's love. The devil will begin to plant thoughts in your head that it's your fault. He will try to convince you that you have to do more in order to get your healing. God never withholds healing because of our lack of obedience. Healing is not based on our actions, but on His. We don't act to receive healing; we act because we have been healed.

Chapter 20

Deal With the Root Cause

One important thing to remember is that you can't separate faith from being led by the Holy Spirit. Everything we believe and do flows from our relationship with God. He knows every area of our lives. He is able to guide us through life and point us in the direction we need to go. He knows the most important areas to deal with first. You may need to deal with the root cause of your sickness before you can receive healing. God knows how to get to the core issues in order for you to receive and keep your healing. Let's look at another man Jesus healed.

> *Now it happened on a certain day, as He was teaching, that there were Pharisees and teachers of the law sitting by, who had come out of every town of Galilee, Judea, and Jerusalem. And the power of the Lord was present to heal them. Then behold, men brought on a bed a man who was paralyzed, whom they sought to bring in and lay before Him. And when they could not find how they might bring him in, because of the crowd, they went up on the housetop and let him down with his bed through the tiling into the midst before Jesus. When He saw their faith, He said to him, "Man, your sins are forgiven you." And the scribes and the Pharisees began to reason, saying, "Who is this who speaks blasphemies? Who can forgive sins but God alone?" But when Jesus perceived their thoughts, He answered and said to them, "Why are you reasoning in your hearts? Which is easier, to say, 'Your sins are forgiven you,' or to say, 'Rise up and walk'? But that you may know that the Son of Man has*

power on earth to forgive sins"—He said to the man who was paralyzed, "I say to you, arise, take up your bed, and go to your house." Immediately he rose up before them, took up what he had been lying on, and departed to his own house, glorifying God.

Luke 5:17-25

It was obvious that this man needed to be healed. Jesus didn't need a sign from heaven to see that he couldn't walk. But He did need a word from God regarding the root cause. Apparently, this man didn't believe he was forgiven. This meant he felt that his paralysis was the punishment for his sins. Instead of just healing the man and sending him on his way, Jesus changed his life. Being able to walk again was a miracle; being forgiven by God was an even greater blessing.

In order for this man to be healed, he needed to deal with a deeper issue. Until he knew that he was forgiven, it was going to be difficult to receive healing. That's why we need to be led by the Holy Spirit. If we are asking for healing and He says to forgive someone, we need to do that first so that we can receive our healing. Any delay in the manifestation of healing is not God's plan. He wants you healed today, but sometimes that means dealing with the root in order for the whole tree to be healthy.

So Jesus answered and said to them, "Have faith in God. For assuredly, I say to you, whoever says to this mountain, 'Be removed and be cast into the sea,' and does not doubt in his heart, but believes that those things he says will be done, he will have whatever he says. Therefore I say to you, whatever things you ask when you pray, believe that you receive them, and you will have them. "And whenever you stand praying, if you have anything against anyone, forgive him, that your Father in heaven may also forgive you your trespasses.

But if you do not forgive, neither will your Father in heaven forgive your trespasses."

Mark 11:22-26

Verses 25 and 26 are connected to verses 22-24. These verses are some of the greatest words on faith that you will find, but you can't forget to deal with the heart issues. If you ignore them, your faith won't work like it's supposed to. God doesn't want you to die sick, but dying sick won't keep you from going to heaven. If you let unforgiveness take root in your heart, it is worse than sickness; it could actually separate you from the love of God and cause you to turn your back on Him and not go to heaven.

Your physical condition is often times a reflection of your inward man. Bitterness, anger, and regrets can be the root cause of sickness. God knows that your spirit has to be whole in order for your body to thrive, so He made a way for you to be free from emotional hurts as well.

Surely He has borne our griefs and carried our sorrows; yet we esteemed Him stricken, smitten by God, and afflicted. But He was wounded for our transgressions, He was bruised for our iniquities; the chastisement for our peace was upon Him, and by His stripes we are healed.

Isaiah 53:4-5

Jesus bore all of our burdens, and if we can learn how to let go of all the things that caused us pain, scars, sadness, regrets, shame, and anger, we will be able to receive healing. These weights we are carrying were taken by Jesus, and we are not able to bare this load. They can be enormous, far greater than our ability. God never intended for us to be laden down with these griefs and sorrows. Jesus wants you to give them to Him. His burden is light and there is no strain.

God created us to be dependent on Him. We are His creation, and He never intended for us to find our own way or figure out how to fix ourselves. Jesus suffered and died for all our sickness, disease, and hurts. He took our place. He wants us to come to Him for help. He is much greater than we will ever be. Cast your cares on Him for He cares for you (1 Peter 5:7).

Chapter 21

Ways to Receive Healing

The Gifts of the Spirit

There is more than one way to receive healing. The gifts of the Spirit mentioned in 1 Corinthians 12 include word of knowledge, working of miracles, and gifts of healings. Many people have been healed through these gifts. All of these are distributed as the Holy Spirit desires, and oftentimes, they are a demonstration of what is available to anyone who believes.

We don't live our daily lives depending on the gifts of the Spirit. We have the Holy Spirit in us. All we have to do is act on the Word of God, with His direction, and receive His promises. Healing already belongs to us, so we don't have to wait for a special manifestation to receive it. Unbelievers and Christians who are not knowledgeable of God's promises are the ones who most often receive healing through the Gifts of the Spirit. They don't know God has already healed them. God demonstrates His power through these gifts so that people can see what is available to anyone who believes.

The best way to receive healing is to hear from God, believe His Word, and act on it. This is the method every believer can use. It doesn't require finding someone else to pray for you and you don't have to wait; just turn to God in your heart and receive.

Laying on of Hands

The most common way people receive is through a transfer of anointing by touch. The laying on of hands and prayer cloths are examples of how the anointing can be transferred from one to another.

> *When the sun was setting, all those who had any that were sick with various diseases brought them to Him; and He laid His hands on every one of them and healed them.*
>
> *Luke 4:40*

> *And He laid His hands on her, and immediately she was made straight, and glorified God.*
>
> *Luke 13:13*

> *And it happened that the father of Publius lay sick of a fever and dysentery. Paul went in to him and prayed, and he laid his hands on him and healed him.*
>
> *Acts 28:8*

> *Now God worked unusual miracles by the hands of Paul, so that even handkerchiefs or aprons were brought from his body to the sick, and the diseases left them and the evil spirits went out of them.*
>
> *Acts 19:11-12*

The anointing comes from the Holy Spirit in us. When contact is made, there is an actual transfer of healing power. It goes from the minister to the one being touched. God's power goes into them and begins to drive out sickness and restore their body. The minister has to be confident that God's power will flow through them. The receiver needs to have faith that the anointing is going into them and will change their circumstances.

Now a certain woman had a flow of blood for twelve years, and had suffered many things from many physicians. She had spent all that she had and was no better, but rather grew worse. When she heard about Jesus, she came behind Him in the crowd and touched His garment. For she said, "If only I may touch His clothes, I shall be made well." Immediately the fountain of her blood was dried up, and she felt in her body that she was healed of the affliction. And Jesus, immediately knowing in Himself that power had gone out of Him, turned around in the crowd and said, "Who touched My clothes?" But His disciples said to Him, "You see the multitude thronging You, and You say, 'Who touched Me?' " And He looked around to see her who had done this thing. But the woman, fearing and trembling, knowing what had happened to her, came and fell down before Him and told Him the whole truth. And He said to her, "Daughter, your faith has made you well. Go in peace, and be healed of your affliction."

Mark 5:25-34

This woman had faith before she ever made contact with Jesus. She made it clear, "If I can touch His clothes, I will be whole." She had faith that He had the power to heal her, and when she touched His clothes, that power would come into her. Now, she wasn't focused on the power; she was looking to Jesus.

The transfer of anointing is only one of the ways to receive from Jesus. The answer isn't the act of touching; the answer is connecting with Jesus. When you are being ministered to, don't look to see if your body is changing, focus on Jesus. We are healed by Jesus, not our actions. We act because we have faith in Him.

Anointing with Oil

> *Is anyone among you sick? Let him call for the elders of the church, and let them pray over him, anointing him with oil in the name of the Lord. And the prayer of faith will save the sick, and the Lord will raise him up. And if he has committed sins, he will be forgiven. Confess your trespasses to one another, and pray for one another, that you may be healed. The effective, fervent prayer of a righteous man avails much.*
>
> *James 5:14-16*

James wrote that anyone sick should call the elders of the church and ask them to anoint him with oil. This is another way to receive healing. You should note that it works best when the sick person initiates the interaction. Going to the sick and ministering to them is caring, but it doesn't show any desire or faith on the part of the sick person. It's better if they call the elders and say, "As soon as you pray, I'll receive my healing."

Anointing with oil is not what heals the sick; it's the prayer of faith that heals. Anointing with oil marks a specific time when the anointing was transferred and action was taken to receive healing. It was the moment everyone released their faith so the sick person could be healed. It was the declaration of faith in God's healing provision that actually released healing in the individual.

You Can Heal the Sick

And He said to them, "Go into all the world and preach the gospel to every creature. He who believes and is baptized will be saved; but he who does not believe will be condemned. And these signs will follow those who believe: In My name they will cast out demons; they will speak with new tongues; they will take up serpents; and if they drink anything deadly, it will by no means hurt them; they will lay hands on the sick, and they will recover."

Mark 16:15-18

Jesus said that every believer can lay hands on the sick and see them get healed. You don't have to be saved a long time, have a degree from Bible school, or be an elder in your church; you can minister to the sick if you believe. He also said we can cast out demons like He did.

When the sun was setting, all those who had any that were sick with various diseases brought them to Him; and He laid His hands on every one of them and healed them. And demons also came out of many, crying out and saying, "You are the Christ, the Son of God!" And He, rebuking them, did not allow them to speak, for they knew that He was the Christ.

Luke 4:40-41

How God anointed Jesus of Nazareth with the Holy Spirit and with power, who went about doing good and healing all who were oppressed by the devil, for God was with Him.

Acts 10:38

Satan is the source of sickness. Diseases came when sin entered the earth. Before sin, there was perfect health. Jesus cast demons from people and they were healed. Not every sickness is caused by a demon, nor is every sick person demon-possessed. The devil oppresses people with sickness and disease. Jesus gave us authority over the devil and everything he causes, so when we rebuke the devil, people will be healed.

Chapter 22

Jesus Gave Us Authority

The key to casting out demons is to know that you have authority through the name of Jesus. In Mark 16:17, Jesus said, *"In My name they will cast out demons."* Jesus gave us authority over all the works of the devil by using His name. Authority is not power; it's permission to use someone else's power. The power comes from God, and we access that power by using the name of Jesus. Every time we speak in His name, He backs up what we say and causes it to come to pass. He gave us authority because He wants us to use it, and Jesus taught us how to use authority over sickness.

> *And behold, one of the rulers of the synagogue came, Jairus by name. And when he saw Him, he fell at His feet and begged Him earnestly, saying, "My little daughter lies at the point of death. Come and lay Your hands on her, that she may be healed, and she will live." ...Then He took the child by the hand, and said to her, "Talitha, cumi," which is translated, "Little girl, I say to you, arise." Immediately the girl arose and walked, for she was twelve years of age. And they were overcome with great amazement.*
>
> *Mark 5:22-23, 41-42*

The girl was healed when Jesus spoke. He spoke with authority expecting her to come back to life.

> *Then they brought to Him one who was deaf and had an impediment in his speech, and they begged Him to put*

His hand on him. And He took him aside from the multitude, and put His fingers in his ears, and He spat and touched his tongue. Then, looking up to heaven, He sighed, and said to him, "Ephphatha," that is, "Be opened." Immediately his ears were opened, and the impediment of his tongue was loosed, and he spoke plainly.

Mark 7:32-35

You may think that this man was healed when Jesus touched his ears and tongue, but actually he was healed when Jesus said to him, "Be opened." The man was deaf so Jesus touched his ears and tongue to show him what He was about to do. The actual healing came when Jesus used His authority.

Now He arose from the synagogue and entered Simon's house. But Simon's wife's mother was sick with a high fever, and they made request of Him concerning her. So He stood over her and rebuked the fever, and it left her. And immediately she arose and served them.

Luke 4:38-39

When Jesus ministered to Simon's mother-in-law, He didn't address her, He rebuked the fever. He spoke directly to the sickness, and it left. When you use your delegated authority, don't talk to God or the person, speak directly to the sickness. God has already dealt with the devil, and Jesus already bought freedom from oppression for every one of us, so we don't need to talk to God about it. If we see someone sick, we need to use our authority, rebuke the sickness, and command it to leave. Jesus said that using our authority demonstrates great faith.

Now when Jesus had entered Capernaum, a centurion came to Him, pleading with Him, saying, "Lord, my servant is lying at home paralyzed, dreadfully tormented." And Jesus said to him, "I will come and heal him." The centurion answered and said, "Lord, I am not worthy that You should come under my roof. But only speak a word, and my servant will be healed. For I also am a man under authority, having soldiers under me. And I say to this one, 'Go,' and he goes; and to another, 'Come,' and he comes; and to my servant, 'Do this,' and he does it." When Jesus heard it, He marveled, and said to those who followed, "Assuredly, I say to you, I have not found such great faith, not even in Israel!

Matthew 8:5-10

The centurion demonstrated faith because he understood authority. When you are given authority, you are expected to use it. You have to trust that the one who gave you authority will support you when you exercise it.

Behold, I give you the authority to trample on serpents and scorpions, and over all the power of the enemy, and nothing shall by any means hurt you.

Luke 10:19

Jesus gave us authority over all the works of the devil, so—nothing will hurt us. If we believe in Him and trust His word, we can rebuke the devil, and he will flee. Jesus gave us authority so we can heal the sick with confidence.

And Jesus said to him, "I will come and heal him."

Matthew 8:7

Jesus didn't say, "I will come pray for him." He said, "I will heal him." This is confidence in the power that comes with authority. Jesus was doing the will of the Father. He wasn't waiting to see if the Father was willing; He knew He was willing to heal. Jesus was actively causing God's will to be carried out because He knew He had authority over sickness and disease. We need to use the name of Jesus with authority. Don't ask God if He wants this person well; use your delegated authority and heal them.

God spoke to me and said, "Stop praying for the sick and start healing the sick." Praying for the sick means blessing them and hoping something happens; healing the sick means getting them well. Now, every time I minister to a sick person, I speak with authority. I command the sickness to leave, life to come, and I tell their body to be healed.

Instead of asking the sick person, "What do you need prayer for?" Find out what they are believing for. Ask, "What are you expecting to happen when we pray?" This takes their eyes off the problem and gets them looking at the solution. Faith expects something to happen. By having them think about being healed, you get them expecting. Instead of rehearsing all of their problems, now they are talking about being healed.

Chapter 23

Staying Healed

Kenneth Hagin ministered to many thousands of people over the course of seventy years. When talking to the people that had been healed, he told them to watch out for the "counter attack." In war, if you push the enemy back, you have to make sure that he doesn't wait for a while then attack you again. The devil lost the battle when you received your healing. He will wait until you are at a weak moment and bring the symptoms back on you. He also whispers in your head, "See, you're not healed," but—this is a lie!

The devil wants to oppress you keep you oppressed. He will lie to you about receiving your healing. He will say things like, "It was a trick. You never got it. You don't deserve it. You're still sick." All of these are lies. He is trying to get you to give up your faith and believe that you are still sick.

> *Therefore submit to God. Resist the devil and he will flee from you.*
>
> *James 4:7*

Go back to the truths that got you healed. Say with your mouth, "I am healed by Jesus!" Don't let the devil's thoughts and worries play in your head. The best way to stay free is to resist it immediately and emphatically. Don't wait until the thoughts take root. Deal with them, with authority, as soon as they come.

I was healed of back pain in February of 1992. A month later I was working in the back yard, and my back began to hurt. It was hard work that could cause anyone discomfort. I stood up and said, "Devil! I was healed a month ago, and I refuse to allow you to put that pain back on me!" Instantly, all pain left.

> But I beg you that when I am present I may not be bold with that confidence by which I intend to be bold against some, who think of us as if we walked according to the flesh. For though we walk in the flesh, we do not war according to the flesh. For the weapons of our warfare are not carnal but mighty in God for pulling down strongholds, casting down arguments and every high thing that exalts itself against the knowledge of God, bringing every thought into captivity to the obedience of Christ,
>
> *2 Corinthians 10:2-5*

We can stay healed by resisting the devil and all the thoughts he puts in our mind.

> For the word of God is living and powerful, and sharper than any two-edged sword, piercing even to the division of soul and spirit, and of joints and marrow, and is a discerner of the thoughts and intents of the heart.
>
> *Hebrews 4:12*

The Word helps us determine what is true and what is a lie. The Holy Spirit will teach you how to know the difference. Spend time in God's Word while you are healthy and especially if you are sick. Focus on the passages that teach on healing. Let them produce faith in your heart. Turn your heart to Jesus, expect Him to help, and receive your healing.

Here's How to Pray

If you are ready to receive your healing say this out loud:

> *Jesus, thank you for taking all sickness and pain. I receive healing in my body right now. I have Your life flowing through me.*
>
> *Devil, I command you to leave in the name of Jesus! You cannot oppress me any longer! I am free by the stripes of Jesus!*
>
> *Sickness and pain, I command you to leave, now, in Jesus' name!*
>
> *Body (or you can speak to the part of your body that is sick — back, knee, heart...), be whole! Be restored!*
>
> *I am healed!*
>
> *I am whole!*

About the Author

Dan and Veronica Bean began ministering in 1995 in their local church. They taught in the church Bible school and were co-hosts for a weekly radio broadcast for fifteen years. In 2005 they pioneered a church in Wesley Chapel, Florida. Four years later they closed the church and began preparing for a traveling ministry.

Their European ministry began in 2013 in Istanbul, Turkey. The next year they began ministry in Slovenia and the former Yugoslavia. Beloved International was launched in January 2015 and the ministry has exploded since then. Their current ministry takes them to over fifty churches in Southeast Europe, reaching into twelve countries.

Divine healing has always been a major part of their ministry. Both were healed by God at a very young age. Growing up in godly homes, they were taught to trust Jesus as their healer. Now, their ministry includes teaching and preaching on God's will for all to be healed. Their goal is to raise up an army of believers that know how to use their authority over sickness and disease.

Printed in Great Britain
by Amazon